THE MAN WHO WOULD BE KING
CHARLES III

FROM WILLIAM THE CONQUEROR TO A PROPER CHARLIE!
A WHIMSICAL TALE OF BRITISH ROYALTY

MARTIN KILLIPS

First published in 2023 by Kinetic Publishing

This book contains satirical commentaries of historical and current events going back a thousand years. Some readers may not share this sense of humour nor the opinions expressed by the artist. To understand editorial cartoons and content it is important to understand their effectiveness as a counterweight to power. It is presumed readers approach satire with a broad-minded foundation and healthy knowledge of objective facts of the subjects depicted.

This is a work of satire. It is based in reality. It is not intended to be a work of historical non-fiction that presents all of the facts. Other people's views of events and figures may differ.

Definitely not official!

No part of this book may be reproduced, or stored in a retrieval system, or transmitted in any form or by any means, electronic, mechanical, photocopying, recording, or otherwise, without express written permission of the author/illustrator.

Illustrations: Martin Killips
Editor: Michaela Killips
Visual Editor: Harriet Killips
Cover design by: Pankaj Runthala

 A catalogue record for this book is available from the National Library of Australia

Copyright © 2023 Martin Killips

All rights reserved.

ISBN: 978-0-6486844-0-4 (Paperback)
ISBN: 978-0-6486844-1-1 (eBook)

THIS BOOK IS DEDICATED TO MICHAEL JEROME DENNEHY

I first met Michael Jerome Dennehy in 1988 when he ran the duty-free operation at a major airport in the UK. At the time he was obliged to be nice to me as I worked for the overseeing airport authority. After I resigned and moved on, he was no longer under any such obligation but he still invited me to partake in splendiferous lunches and dinners on the company card and provided me the occasional bottle of Krug Champagne and the best Cuban cigars money could buy as well as fix all manner of shady dealings to assist me when I fell on lean times and my mortgage was due.

Michael grew up in Dublin in the 1930s, a time of great social and political upheaval in Ireland. As a young lad he knew and regularly crossed paths with the great Irish statesman Eamon de Valera, who prayed at the same church on Sundays. Before running the duty-free operation at the airport in the 1980s, he spent a lifetime travelling the world managing some of the most exclusive hotels in exotic locations. His worldly travels not only filled Michael with sagacity, they also ensured he always has an amusing anecdote to share for every situation, and some deeply philosophical insight to impart in his soft, lilting, Irish brogue. A friend and father figure to boot, my life is richer for knowing him.

WHY THE BEAR?

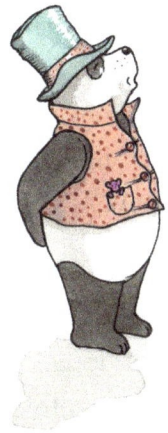

Long before I became a writer I was a portrait artist. Not an artist of any renown, but I was sufficiently competent to earn a decent living drawing portraits of people, dogs, cats, horses – indeed anything where I could earn a crust!

In the early 1990s I discovered by pure chance that I had a knack for writing silly rhymes. Many of the rhymes featured a bear – perhaps because 'bear' is an easy word to rhyme. However, as I was unfamiliar with drawing cartoon bears at that point, I set about learning how. My inspiration was Ernest Shepard whose illustrations are legendary. I chose a panda rather than brown bear or teddy bear for my main character because the black and white colouring encapsulated the polarised views I often wove into many of my poems.

I styled the early versions of my panda on still life drawings I made of Chi Chi, whose stuffed remains are kept in a glass case in London's Natural History Museum. I combined these still life drawings with Shepard's sketching style and The Big Bamboo was born.

In **The Man Who Would Be King Charles III** I have decorated the book with sketches of The Big Bamboo in various Royal guises. I decided to retain the use of his character because he adds a softness and comical air, not so apparent with lifelike renditions – plus after 30+ years, I find him easy to draw!

M.K.

PREFACE

Britain's Royal families have possessed every human characteristic from kindness and perceptive visionary to the lesser traits like pinchpenny, lecherous wastrel (some even worse than Andrew!) and even cold-blooded murderer. **The Man Who Would Be King Charles III** summarises every Royal bottom that's sat on the throne from William the Conqueror in 1066 through to Charles III. It is a tongue in cheek journey, in rhyming couplets, through Britain's last thousand years of Royals supported throughout with amusing illustrations. If you thought history was dull at school, you need to read this book. For this is a factual work based on fiction – or is it fiction based on facts?! Either way, it will amuse you and might even trigger a deeper interest in learning more about British history.

I first sat down to write this poem in late August of 1997. At the time Elizabeth II was on the throne and

Princess Diana was still alive. My intention was to write a short poem, preferably less than thirty lines, that listed all the Kings and Queens of England (or as it evolved, the United Kingdom) in chronological order from 1066 to the present day. The poem's main purpose was to serve as an aide-memoire. However, after typing the first thirty lines and discovering I'd barely covered the reign of William the Conqueror I realised my original intention had faltered. As is common in life, the 'failure' spawned a new idea…I could, instead, write a much longer but equally irreverent poetic summary of British Royalty and include highlights of their respective reigns. Once I committed to writing a more expansive poetic history of the Royals, I worked feverishly, like a man possessed for three days and nights, completing it around midnight on the 30th of August 1997. The following day I heard of Princess Diana's untimely death in Paris. After adjusting to the shocking news, I knew the poem would require updating. Of course, when Queen Elizabeth passed away in 2022 this poem once more required amending. In truth, whilst Britain retains its monarchy this work will need to be added to. I have merely covered the first thousand years. When Charlie goes and William takes over, if I am not around, someone else will need to add a verse or two – and so too when William passes the throne to his eldest child, George, and beyond. **The Man**

ᙏ PREFACE ᘓ

Who Would Be King Charles III, which started life as a poetic aide-memoire now runs to over 600 lines and some 3,300 words. The poem has grown into something many times larger than the original idea in my head. But in a sense, this rhyme will never be complete for it is not so much a work, as a work in progress. It has also been one of the most enjoyable tales to write, combining my love of history with my penchant for whimsical rhymes. I sincerely hope you enjoy reading it as much as I enjoyed writing it.

Martin Killips, April 2023

LIST OF BRITAIN'S MONARCHS AFTER BATTLE OF HASTINGS 1066

House of Normandy:

William I (the Conqueror) 1066-1087
William II 1087-1100
Henry I 1100-1135
Stephen 1135-1154
Henry II 1154-1189
Richard I (the Lionheart) 1189-1199
John I 1199-1216

House of Plantagenet:

Henry III 1216-1272
Edward I (Longshanks) 1272-1307
Edward II 1307-1327
Edward III 1327-1377
Richard II 1377-1399
Henry IV 1399-1413
Henry V 1413-1422
Henry VI 1422-1461 and 1470-1471
Edward IV 1461-70 and 1471-1483
Edward V 1483-1483
Richard III 1483-1485

House of Tudor:

Henry VII 1485-1509
Henry VIII 1509-1547
Edward VI 1547-1553
Mary I 1553-1558
Elizabeth I 1558-1603

House of Stuart:

James I (and VI) 1603-1625
Charles I 1625-1649
Interregnum
Charles II 1660-1685
James II 1685-1688
William III and Mary II 1688-1702, 1688-1694
Anne 1702-1714

House of Hanover:

George I 1714-1727
George II 1727-1760
George III 1760-1820
George IV 1820-1830
William IV 1830-1837
Victoria 1837-1901
Edward VII 1901-1910

House of Windsor:

George V 1910-1936
Edward VIII 1936-1936
George VI 1936-1952
Elizabeth II 1952-2022
Charles III 2022 -

IN THE BEGINNING…

The Kings and Queens who've ruled our land
can sometimes be confusing;
For knowing who they are and when
can take some real perusing.

We start this tale way back in time
to when King Harold reigned;
Till Bill from Normandy arrived
and Harold's power waned;
The place and year this war occurred
was Hastings, Ten, Six, Six;
They bashed each other all day long
with axes, swords and sticks;
The Norman knights attacked the men
of Harold's sturdy army;
Who'd just quick marched from
Stamford Bridge -
they were, of course, quite barmy!

William in full fight!   **1066**

But as the Normans reached the end
of proving their endeavour;
Young Billy had a bright idea
which he thought rather clever;
Pretending to retreat, he told
his knights to flee the field;
And as the English broke their ranks
the knights returned and killed.

So at the ending of the day
young William was the winner;
And those (aerobically) who'd lived
were healthy and much thinner!
Poor Harold lay upon the field,
an arrow in his eye;
Although some say he fell from sword:
but either way - he died.

Harold...wishing he'd stayed in bed!

Then William marched to London Town
  to wake the poor Archbishop;
Demanding that he crown him King
  and serve the spoils with hyssop;
The Bishop sobbed, refused to place
  the crown on Billy's head,
So pushing Bishop to one side
  Bill crowned himself instead!
And Bashing Bill the Conqueror
  ruled twenty years plus one;
Then Rufus Red became the King -
  Bill gave it to his son.

The number thirteen's deemed unlucky,
and so it proved for Red;
A rule of thirteen years before
poor Rufus wound up dead!
A hunting trip in Forests, New -
the aim, to shoot a deer;
A glancing shot flew off a tree,
made Rufus feel quite queer;
But youngest brother Henry
was around to take the throne;

*(Some say a bit too quickly -
from such thoughts are rumours grown).*

Rufus...about to say: "Ouch!"

The year was One, One, double O -
he ruled till thirty Five;
When suddenly one morning
he was not, alas, alive!
His nephew Stephen had a go
but squabbled with Matilda;
A civil war raged for a while
and Stephen almost killed 'er!
Steve won and ruled till Fifty Four
when Matty's eldest nipper,
(Another lad called Henry)
grabbed the rôle of England's skipper;

Stephen and Matilda getting acquainted.

Now Henry was a goodly King -
but rowed with Thomas Becket;[1]
The knights who slaked his fury
didn't live to full regret it!
Our Henry Two remained in charge
till late in Eighty Nine,
When sitting down to luncheon
he went stiff - and didn't dine.

His third son, Richard, had the throne -
became the Lionhearted;
He only lived at home six months -
the rest he was departed!
He spent his time in Palestine
on crusades 'gainst the Moors;
He liked a tan, or may be sand -
who knows what was the cause?

*(This is the time of Robin Hood
and men in tights of green;
The year was now Eleven, Ninety Nine,
as you can glean;).*

1199

Robin sHood be green!

Then England gained a Lackland John,
  a King who wasn't clever;
Who rather made a mess of every
  deed and good endeavour;
His barons forced him to their door,
  to sign the Magna Carta;
He squealed: *"No need to bargain hard -*
  I'll give you all you barter!"
So John took heed at Runnymede
  and lived to Twelve Sixteen;
When eldest son, another Henry,
  played the rôle as Queen!
(Of course I know he was a King -
  but rumour has it so,
That Henry Three was sixty five
  and STILL he didn't know!).

John catching up on his paper work.

Then Edward landed on the throne -
bequeathed the Welsh a Prince,
Regardless of their wishes,
and there's been one ever since!
In Thirteen Seven, Edward sadly
passed along his way;
Then eldest son, another Edward -
Pink, his sobriquet!
He rather liked his Piers and Hugh -
so limp of limb and hem;
Perhaps like Ed they'd also had
some Henry Three in them!

1307

King Ted II, with his Piers and Hugh!

Then Edward Two was Edward Three -
the year was Twenty Seven;
And he aveng-ed Bannockburn,
he claimed, with help from Heaven;
He also kept his mum locked up -
her name was Isabella;
And killed her lover, Mortimer -
a sort of dead nice fella!
He then went on to score a ton -
a Hundred Years' old War;
I'll say this for our Edward Three -
you couldn't call him **bore!**
But bore he was, upon his back -
our Eddy went and died;
The year was Thirteen Seven, Seven -
we lost his tough old hide

And grandson Richard was the King,
  with help from John of Gaunt;
Our King, a silly Dick, because
  our John felt free to flaunt;
Then Richard lost it all whilst touring
  Ireland's emerald isle;
When Henry Bolingbroke came forth -
  and took the throne by guile;
The year was Thirteen Ninety Nine -
  he lasted fourteen years;
And then he passed it on again
  with lots of joyous tears;

The Bard himself was most impressed
and even wrote a play:
*"I know you all and will awhile
uphold your idle way;
Yet herein will I, like the sun,
that doth permit the clouds
To smother up his beauty
from the world when he allows!
If all the year were having fun,
to sport t'would be as work,
But when they seldom come
they wished for come!"* so Prince Hal shirked;
His father, bless him, Henry Four,
thought Hal an awful waster:
*"Stop messing with your fattish friend -
that lazy Falstaff baster!"*

Prince Hal, soon to be Henry V,
remembering his soliloquy.

But in the end Hal wins the day
and *paid the debt not promised;*
And Henry Four said *"Listen son,
you turned out really honest!
You make a father very proud;
I'll pass my crown to you."*
And so he did, sententiously -
he went and dropped dead too!

Our Henry Five went on to fame,
Upon Saint Crispin's Day;
At Agincourt he stopped the French
with stakes put in their way;
The English archers had a ball,
or rather, loads of arrows,
They accidentally killed the French
by shooting up at sparrows!
More than Hamlet, Henry Five,
is Shakespeare's noble champion:
Such verve, élan - a real man's man,
(a movie for Jane Campion?).

Author's note: Even though I thought of this line many years ago it still cracks me up! Apologies for my vanity.

Henry VI attending Show and Tell.

Which brings us up to Henry Six,
a student, most discerning;
His colleges at Eton, Cambridge,
founded for the learning;
But for all his intellect -
a bonus one supposes,
His weakly rule led England to
the Wars of blooming Roses!

Ted IV and Henry VI abusing nature.

He ran the show from Fourteen,
Twenty Two to Sixty One;
But when he started Henry Six
was not much more than none!
He lost it then for nine long years,
to Yorkist, Edward Four;
Then won it back for just a year
but after that, no more.

Then Edward grabbed it back again
at Tewkesbury, north of Gloucester;
And held the crown till Eighty Three
and then he finally lost her!
His son, poor Edward Five,
sat on the throne for not one year;
Then uncle Richard, it's alleged,
made nephew disappear!

The brief home of Edward V -
the Tower of London.

If you've been counting you will know
we're up to Richard Three -
Two years he spent, with his back bent,
till Bosworth did for he!
Then Henry Tudor, Earl of Richmond,
stopped the Roses War;
Proclaimed himself the Seventh Henry
to dispense the law;
He held the crown from Fourteen, Eighty Five
to Fifteen, Nine;
Then as his eldest Arthur died
it passed to next in line;
His second son was once again
a Henry - soon the Eighth;
*(Try rhyming that without a lisp,
and I'll, your fortune, mak'th!).*

We all know Henry had six wives
but wanted just one son;
(Perhaps when he was naked
all his wives would up and run!);
He died in Fifteen, Forty Seven,
obese and broken hearted;
The realm no better off,
than how it was before he started;
At least he left an heir -
Jane Seymour's boy, another Eddy;
Though he was only ten years old
and not, alas, quite ready;
A sickly child, and weakling,
with the scourge of halitosis;
He popped his cork in Fifty Three -
he had tuberculosis!

Henry VIII realising marriage
is about love not happiness!

For just nine days, Ms L Jane Greys
controlled the strings of power;
Then Mary, Edward's sister,
chopped Jane's head off in The Tower;
Now Mary's manic purges
made her rather more contrary;
And to prove this trait was noticed
she was known as Bloody Mary!
But Bloody Mary, quite contrary,
didn't last so long;
Just eight short years of Right Foot fears
then she, at last, was gone.

They didn't have to look too far
for new Queen, sister Lizzie;
They called our Liz, the Virgin Queen -
because she was too busy!
She ruled the land from Fifteen, Fifty Eight
till Sixteen Three;
She liked to tell her courtiers that:
"I did it - just with me!"

For Francis Drake, the sea dog rake,
was rumoured to have kissed her;
If he tried more, we will ignore,
but if he did: he missed her!
At least our Francis kept his head,
indeed, no laughing matter;
Sir Walter Raleigh, with cigar,
left his upon a platter!

Raleigh proving that smoking really can damage your health.

1618

His love for Lizzie knew no bounds
And whilst she lived he thrived
But once she shuffled off her coil
His fortunes soon nosedived!

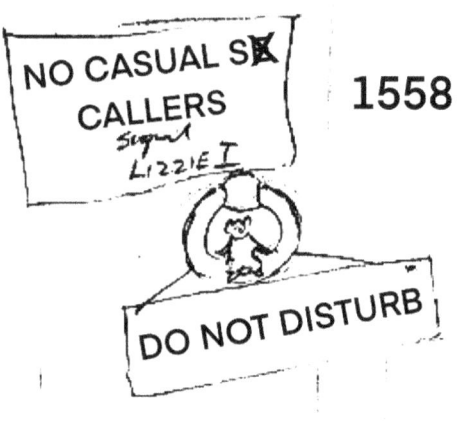

And now we must, move on, discuss
>> the first real Stuart King;
His name was James, a Scottish name,
>> is what I know of him;
He had an Addled Parliament,
>> I think, Sixteen-Fourteen;
It might have been another year -
>> the man was rarely seen!
(How strange that Mr Guy Fawkes
>> *piled his powder to the limit*
In Parliament, to get his man -
>> *for James was never in it!);*
Regardless, James the First, passed onward
>> late in Twenty Five;
And second son, young Charlie came,
>> at least, back then alive.

1605

Perhaps if the barrels were labelled Port instead of Gunpowder, history would have been different.

Now Charles the First,
though not the worst,
booked prayers for Bishops' Wars;
The civil strife throughout his life,
young Cromwell said he caused;
Edgehill, Marston Moor then Naseby,
all, he blamed on Charles;
So when he spanked the naughty King
his yelps were heard for miles!

When waiting at the scaffold,
two shirts buttoned 'gainst the chill,
The executioner said: *"Charles,
don't fear, you'll not get ill!"*
He raised the jagged axe above
his solemn, blacked masked head,
Then quickly brought it down again
and Charles the First was dead!

Charles I, awaits an instant cure for his laryngitis.

From Sixteen, Forty Nine to Sixty
we'd In-Terr-Regg-Num;
Which means that no one was in charge -
but Cromwell and his son!
But after Sixteen, Fifty Eight,
with Cromwell out the way,
The Dec of Breda made it clear
that Richard couldn't stay.

So Charles the Second, with his head,
began the Restoration,
And public houses, theatres too,
reopened for the nation;
The Earl of Clarendon advised,
as Charlie's closest pal;
But Dutch War messing up forced Charles
to start a new Cabal;
And Charles in turn, in Sixteen, Eighty Five
passed it to James,
His second son, and second King
to come by with that name;
His three years ended smartly
with a Glorious Revolution;
But losses at the Boyne and Aughrim
sealed his devolution.

His son-in-law and daughter,
Will and Mary, took the throne;
Though when I say *they took it* -
they still left it all alone;
They shared the veil of power -
well, at least, till Ninety Four,
But a bout of fatal smallpox
and our Mary was no more.

Poor Willy Three went on alone
till Seventeen and Two,
Then Mary's little sister Anne
became the Queen of phew!
For **eighteen** times she was with child,
not one, alas, survived,
And so the Stuart dynasty
could never be revived.

So twelve years later, on her death,
    to meet the court's criterion,
The crown was passed without ado
    to George - a Hanoverian!
Now George the First, he was the worst,
    he couldn't speak a word!
A King *nichts spracken Englisch?*
    Unconditionally absurd!

THE MAN WHO WOULD BE KING CHARLES III

He died in Twenty Seven -
passed the crown on to his son;
At least this George spoke English
and was thought to be more fun;
The last King into battle
when he fought at Dettingen,
And the troops all died like cattle
as they crushed the French again;
He really loved the opera
and would shout: *"Encore! Encore!"*
Then his musical pretensions
fixed a Handel to his door!

In Seventeen Sixty, George, alas,
　　ordained to pass away;
And George the Third, not Frederick, heard
　　that he was King to stay;
And all went well, for one short spell,
　　till Boston had its Party;
Then overnight, the Yanks took fright,
　　and Independence *starty!*

"Some party - this tea's as weak as buffalo pee!"

1773

This was the time of Captain Cook
　　acclaiming every nation,
And islands sparkling, pure and free,
　　about to lose elation;
In Europe, Boney N was romping -
　　scaring half the world;

The other half dependant on just
how the war unfurled;
(It isn't any wonder to me
George the Third went mad -
It might have seemed, how sick his world,
and madness, not so bad);
He passed away in Eighteen Twenty –
Regent George now King;
He'd run the line for years of nine,
so he knew everything;
He also had a secret love
who held the wrong religion;
Instead he married Caroline
but loved her just a smidgen.

Just ten years on, George Four was gone,
    and brother Willy made it;
"The Sailor King!" the crowd would sing,
    whilst Will went out and laid it!

Not just nice boys...bad girls too, love a sailor!

THE MAN WHO WOULD BE KING CHARLES III

Now shifting on, my rude thoughts gone,
  Queen Vic, she was a winner;
Her not amused, and solemn views,
  enchanted every dinner!
She married Cousin Albert,
  from the Saxe-Coburg-Gotha;
And gave him nine young children –
  so he must have got quite far!

1837-1901

"Vicky...instead of names, we should have numbered them!"

A Crisis in the Bedroom Chamber,
  back in Thirty Nine;
And Palmerston instructed
  not to deviate offline!
Her friendship with Disraeli
  made her India's Em-press;

And joy of spanking Gladstone
    made him flee in some distress!
Her happiness was ended
    in the year of Sixty One;
When Albert, love of all her life,
    had closed his eyes and gone;
She resolves to do, thereafter,
    what she ever wants or feels;
Never caring if the other person
    wounds their heart or heals;
And in spite of this demeanour
    she became a mighty hit;
Inspiring myths of stubborn force –
    that British Bulldog grit!

"At least it's warm!"

A time of great invention
and the ruler of the waves;
Excused by good intention –
Britain had so much to say;
Queen Vic moved on, in Nineteen, One,
and Edward Seven came;
As Prince of Wales he'd caused some tales,
(some business with some dame?);
But once in charge, he came of *arge*,
became, indeed, quite popular;
How else describe, his swollen kibe –
with noun or maybe copula?

Let's cast the line from corny rhyme,
and jump to Nineteen, Ten;
With Edward gone we've now moved on
to Five and George again.

He loved his brother's girlfriend –
did the decent thing: got hitched;
Had five sons and a daughter –
(thank the Lord he was quite rich!)
Only four years after starting,
he consents to brooding war;
With the rest of dimming Europe
he is blind to what's in store;
As he learns of tragic battles –
hears the angry guns again,
Casts his eye on Owen's cattle –
sees the bones that once were men;
He endures it with his people,
and lets fall upon his face
The tears that come from sadness,
and the thoughts, they spill, to trace.

1914-1918

In the year of Nineteen Eighteen,
when the war drew to a close,
'Twixt nine million blood-stained crosses,
grew the poppies, row on row;
And the youth had died in Europe,
and a generation gone;
It changed the face of the human race -
and its echo lingers on.

In Nineteen, Thirty Six our George
   departed from this world,
And Edward Eight, with female mate,
   was in, the cauldron, hurled;
He didn't last long, and soon was gone,
   Wal Simpson did for him,
(There's nothing worse than a Queen *diverced* -
   it's fine though for a King!).

So George the Sixth, the second son,
    became the King to be;
He overcame a stammer
    but still spoke, hes-it-ant-ly!
Throughout the war 'gainst Hitler
    he would visit, raise morale;
Lost the Emperor-ship of India -
    (but still loved the Taj Mahal);
The Commonwealth of Nations,
    he both headed and upheld;
And the tears he shed for Roosevelt,
    from a King, unparalleled;
When he himself, in Nineteen, Fifty Two,
    had passed away,
The country mourned this gentle man
    who'd seen us through the fray.

Which brings us through to Lizzie Two,
and soon the very end;
When I say soon, it might be noon -
such scandal to attend!
She married Phil - a pukka Prince,
and had four kids to clutch;
*(Some people say the Royals play
between the sheets - too much!)*
This leads us on to Fergie,
and her infamous, big toe;
And Princess Di, the Queen of hearts,
who liked her Prince to go!
The once Princess will not be queen,
her radiance, now gone;
Though Britain lost its reddest rose
her legend liveth on.

Charlie, Annie, Andrew, Edward –
what a motley crew!
The gutter press' favourite topic –
most of it untrue;
'Cos all the Royals through the ages,
(and we've mentioned many)
Are prone to all the human errors –
murder to pinchpenny!
Gone are the days they were divine,
regarded more as gods;
The Queen and all her family are, (less i) –
just *anthropods!*
The truth is Lizzie tried real hard,
she simply did her best;
If we'd had wealth to match with hers
we'd run away and rest!

She had her annus horribilis,
  when her house burnt down;
And Di and Charlie breaking up
  caused her to further frown;
Anne and Mark did not do well
  and Andrew even worse;
Liz must have had the feeling
that the House of Windsor's cursed!
At least she had two Corgis –
  though one bites the hand or thigh;
(A classic case, in the doggie race –
  one's bitten and two's shy!);
Our Lizzie Two has slipped from view –
  departed, left the fray;
Our longest serving sovereign has now
  gone and passed away.

1992

"My anus hurts horribilis-ly!"

And now the King, I hear you sing,
is Charlie, number Three;
He's waited longer in the wings
than any Prince to be;
He seems much happier these days
since bunking with Camilla;
And how her star has flickered
from ignoble to vanilla!

(I often think that their affair
was one of true romance;
If she'd looked great her public fate
would be reversed, perchance;
But sweet on the eye was Princess Di -
Camilla, like a horse;
'Gainst pretty face in the public's place,
a horse lacks force, of course!)

THE MAN WHO WOULD BE KING CHARLES III

A proper Charlie now, at last,
is on the throne – so plush;
*(I mean the throne which Royals own -
not one you sit 'n flush!).*
And Charlie says he has an eye
for decent architecture;
To prove it he is never slow
to give a Royal lecture!
He's also seen as very Green
and loves the National Trust;
Whilst brother Edward's rather dull
and rarely much discussed;
But sister Anne (now less her man)
has gusto on her side;
And even won some medals
when she nipped off for a ride!

So what's in store for Charlie
after waiting all these years?
Will he become a goodly King
and grow into his ears?
King Charlie is a decent chap,
who'll turn out rather dandy;
I'll say in brief, with some relief -
thank Christ it's not King Andy!

THE END

ABOUT THE AUTHOR

Martin Killips (the one on the left above) was born in Malaysia and raised by monkeys for the first two years of his life. His primary carer was a female gibbon (see actual photo below) that bottle fed and later spoon fed him until his family returned to the UK briefly then moved to Northern Germany. He started primary school in Germany a month shy of being four and by the time he turned five he was a fluent reader. Consequently, when he returned to the UK and found his classmates learning the alphabet and sounding out words, he chose to hide in the school library until he'd read every book on the shelves. It was during these early years he fell in love with history and poetry – something he retained until he won a scholarship to Oakham where his schoolmasters managed to quell any further thirst he had for learning.

At Oakham School he achieved very little apart from notoriety as a class clown and the distinction for being almost expelled more often than any other pupil. He claims his rebellious persona was less a cry for help and more a simple misunderstanding of his humour.

"One term there was a phase where some boys started burning the teachers' notices that had been pinned up on the walls. I never set fire to any of the notes myself as I considered it a foolhardy act lacking in subtlety. I preferred acts of defiance that involved something more. However, when the head boy pinned up a notice stating in capital letters, 'ANYONE FOUND BURNING NOTICES WILL BE EXPELLED' and signed it, 'David Alloway - Head Boy', the temptation became too much. I removed the note and very carefully burnt it, taking great care to leave Alloway's words scorched but still clearly legible and then pinned it back up in the same spot. A day later all Hell was let loose. Classes were cancelled for the day and all pupils confined to their studies whilst a huge enquiry was launched. It became self-evident that Head boy David Alloway, Housemaster 'Dickie' Davies and Headmaster John Buchanan didn't find the act as amusing as I did. I only managed to escape expulsion by resorting to barefaced lying – a skill acquired and much practised in British public schools, which serves its exponents well in later life, particularly if they venture into politics!"

Leaving Oakham with few qualifications Martin had a brief spell at North London Polytechnic where he studied Philosophy but soon dropped out and took up a job making horseshoes. After a few months he grew tired of hitting hot metal with a hammer and became an estimator's assistant for a civil engineering company. He describes this job as something akin to a living death, and to ensure he was in fact still alive he started racing motorcycles at weekends – an expensive pursuit.

Attending a three day fighter pilot selection process for the Royal Air Force, solely because it paid loss of earnings compensation, he was astounded to find after the three days ended he was the only candidate left standing from an initial draft of one hundred and fifty. It was an achievement made all the more remarkable because Martin did not possess the 20:20 vision required to be a fighter pilot. Fortunately, whilst he was waiting to have his eyes tested he memorised the letters on the bottom line of the eye chart.

Sadly, with poor eyesight, his flying career only lasted two years. A close encounter with a Weetabix truck as he came into land one morning soon led to Martin finding himself back in civvy street.

It was at this point in his life he decided to develop his drawing skills and he was soon making a decent living from intricate pencil drawings of pets, children and indeed anything that sat still long enough. A last minute trip to Northern France to visit the grave of a Great Uncle killed in the Great War triggered his latent interest in history which shortly grew into an obsession. Three years later he returned to Northern France and toured many of the battlefields and visited dozens of the Commonwealth War Grave cemeteries tracing the final resting place of many of the people he'd read about. Importantly, with no schoolmasters about, his interest in history continued to blossom.

Martin emigrated to Australia in 1992 where he discovered, by pure chance, he could write whimsical stories and rhymes. His first picture book, The Big

ABOUT THE AUTHOR

Bamboo, featuring the eponymous panda bear was published in Australia in 1997. Since then he has had five collections of children's poetry published plus many articles and further poems published in D-Mag for Kids. He has also featured on numerous radio shows in Australia reciting his poetry, which was once described by the writer and broadcaster, Phillip Adams, as 'funny, ingenious and somewhat subversive.'

That description by Phillip Adams perfectly encapsulates **The Man Who Would Be King Charles III**. This book is Martin's first publication for adults.

www.martinkillips.com

www.ingramcontent.com/pod-product-compliance
Lightning Source LLC
Chambersburg PA
CBHW070311010526
44107CB00056B/2565